RV CHUCKLES
and
CHUCKHOLES-
The
CONFESSIONS OF
HAPPY CAMPERS

To Lenn,

Congratulations on winning this for doing a good deed at Boonerville.

DARLENE MILLER

Darlene Miller

RV CHUCKLES AND CHUCKHOLES-
THE CONFESSIONS OF HAPPY CAMPERS

This book is written as a humorous and thoughtful commentary of the RV lifestyle. Sometimes solutions may be offered. The publisher and writer and contributors are not engaged in giving financial, or professional services. If you need legal or expert assistance, you need to get a competent professional. The author and publisher shall have neither the liability nor responsibility to any person or entity with respect to loss or damage caused, or alleged to be caused, directly, by information contained in this book.

Many of the names and personal information have been changed so no one will be embarrassed.

RV Chuckles and Chuckholes-
The Confessions of Happy Campers

Dedicated to
all the RV friends
who gave me information to use in this book.
Many names have been changed to prevent
embarrassment.

A Special Dedication
to
my husband
Terry R. Miller
whose love of wanderlust equals mine.
He has enabled me to travel and is a faithful
companion and friend.

Contents

Chapter One

They Don't Understand Us

We lived in a scheduled world and hardly saw each other. Terry went to work at 7 am while I went to work at 3 pm. As an engineer and writer of software and as a nurse, our lives were ordered by timetables and documents. Vacations were the only time we had to forget the clock. Even then, we had to spend days getting to our destination, with a few days at our vacation spot and then hurry back to our jobs.

We decided to take a leave of absence from our jobs and drive a pickup and slide-in camper to Alaska to try out the RV lifestyle.

My parents thought that we were too young to retire to RVing. They weren't even retired yet. Others thought that it would be too expensive and we would be back to work in a couple of years. Wouldn't we miss all the conveniences of our home? Wouldn't we get lonely? How could you spend 24 hours a day and 7 days a week with your partner? What do you do all day? How do you get involved with other people?

This book answers these questions from my point of view and the stories of RV people I have met.

We joined the high tech gypsies, people with hitch-itch, people who spend their children's inheritance, semi-affluent street people, snowbirds, and winter Texans.

In contrast to people who wake up to alarm clocks, start and stop work after whistles, and eat after hearing the dinner bell; we don't know what time it is.

We usually know if it is Monday or Tuesday but don't know if it is the fifth or sixth of the month.

———

Some people seem to think that we are lost and have never found our way home.

———

After a year away from our former home, the people from our bank asked if we had just returned from vacation.

———

I said that we were leaving for a trip to Texas when a friend asked, "Are you packed yet?" She does not understand that our clothes are in the closet. Our dishes and food are in the cupboards. Our medicines and cosmetics are in the bathroom. We pull in the slide, lift the jacks, disconnect from the water, electricity and sewer. We turn on the engine and go.

Things People Say That Prove They Don't Understand Us Rvers

When are you coming home? The last place we lived, before we became fulltimers, was Raleigh, North Carolina. Our friends from Raleigh ask that question. Most of my family live in Iowa. They ask when we are coming home. Our address is in Texas. Once they even put up Christmas stockings in the clubhouse with our names on them because they knew we were coming home for Christmas.

"We did not make reservations. How did you know we would be here?" I inquired.

"Your son sent a package to you," the manager explained.

The first time that I heard the phrase "Home is where you park it," was in a publication written by Kay Peterson. She is a founder of the Escapees RV Club. I like that phrase.

———

"Wouldn't you like to sleep in a real bed? Where do they think we sleep?"

———

After leaving a campground, the teenager took our pass and wished us a "safe drive home." I wanted to tell her that I was already home but I didn't.

Things That You Never Tell Your Homebound Friends

"I slept at Wal-mart last night." They will never understand how you spent over 100 thousand dollars on an RV and then park it overnight at Wal-mart.

"Our RV sleeps eight." " Why?" So you can bring your four kids and stay for a week or two but my RV will never be the same again. You will have to step over someone to go to the bathroom. Their teenager will not understand that they have to rise at 7a.m. so I can make the bed into a table to serve breakfast.

"Yes, you can take a shower now. I'll do the dishes later." They waste water. They don't understand that you have a six-gallon hot water heater.

"Yes, it would be helpful if you make breakfast." They don't understand that you can't make coffee, toast, and microwave sausage at the same time that the air conditioning is on with a 20 or 30 amps circuit.

You run out of things to talk about to your homebound friends after a couple of days. They do not relate to your life style. They are still worried about what the neighbors will say.

After you have heard for the third time about their ills, their children, their clubs, and their jobs, it is time for you to move away from them.

Even my computer doesn't like the word "RVing." It suggests that I want another word such as raving, riving, (what is a rive?) roving or ruining. Should I rev my motor as I rave about roving? That is too much.

Chapter Two

Moving Your RV

B efore you move your RV, there are certain things that you must do.

1.Put down the lid on the commode. You do not want to hear it fall. It is really advisable not to move with the black tank full.

2. Close the refrigerator door. We were sitting with Mary around the campfire when she told us the story of when the refrigerator door was not latched.

"I was in a hurry as I put the chicken casserole into the refrigerator. We were on our way to a family reunion where we were going to show off our new RV. In a contruction zone, Pete made a sudden turn over a rough road. The refrigerator door opened. Out flew the casserole onto the floor. A ketchup bottle plopped upside down over the casserole contents. A dozen eggs was next to land on the floor. Our poodle,

Tootsie, was the only one who was happy. She had a feast."

"We put Tootsie into the back of the pickup until we came to a rest stop to bathe her. (It did not seem fair that she was the first one to use our new shower/tub combination.) Pete scooped up the mess on the floor. Then we had the refrigerator and the floor to clean. I passed the mirror on the wall and could not help laughing at the sight of egg in my hair."

"I wondered how many people used the rest stop area to shower in their RV."

"After changing our clothes, we were on our way but we were an hour and a half late for the family reunion. Our contributions to the meal were hot dogs and potato chips which no one ate because they were eating dessert."

Mary's eyes twinkled as she thought of the family's reaction. "My in-laws thought we were crazy."

3. Be sure that your partner is on board. My husband actually left me once. We had stopped for fuel. I washed the windshield while Terry was putting fuel in the RV. I was returning the cleaning wand to the liquid container when I noticed the RV taking off without me. Fortunately, he did soon miss me, however, and returned for me.

———

Cathy told us about her Rving father, Bill. One day Bill got very muddy as he checked the tires in preparation to move to another location. He told his wife that he was about to get into the RV and clean up.

"When you hear the door close, pull out," he ordered her.

She did as she was told. About fifty miles down the road, a policeman stopped her.

"Did you forget something?" he asked.

"No." She replied.

"Do you have a husband?"

"Yes, he is in the RV," She answered.

"You had better look again," the policeman responded.

Inside the RV, there was no Bill. He was nude in the police car.

Bill explained that he had taken off his muddy clothes outside the RV and thrown them into the RV, at which point the door had closed and his wife had taken off, leaving him sitting on the side of the road without a wallet, phone or clothes.

———

Two women were discussing their next RV trip. "I'm going to Yellowstone National Park," Jean explained.

"Don't forget Old Faithful." Joan replied.

Jean answered, "Oh, he is going with me."

YOU MOVE

If you are using your generator for 20 hours a day, you move to a campground with electricity.

If a forest fire or hurricane is predicted, you move your RV to a safer area.

If the neighbor's dog is barking all night, you move your home.

If you have spent two weeks with your grandchildren and you both are tired of "Mom doesn't do it that way", you move your house.

If you talk to your grandchild on the phone and feel you want to hold him or hug her, it is time to move close to them.

If it is January and the RV, Rock and Gem Show, and the Flea Markets are being held in Quartzsite, Arizona, it is time to move.

If it is February and it is cold where you are located, you move your RV further south.

If it is March and the bluebonnets are blooming, it is time to move to the hill country of Texas or move west to see the desert bloom in Arizona and California.

If it is April and your snowbird friends are moving north, you move your rig north to see your family.

YOU MOVE

If it is May and you want to see a Tulip Festival, it is time to travel to Pella, Iowa or Holland, Michigan. If you want to see a NASCAR race on Memorial Day weekend, you travel to Indiana.

If it is June and your daughter or grandchild is getting married, you move to her hometown.

If it is July and you want to go to the family reunion, it is time to move on.

If it is August and you want to have a chance to take your grandson fishing before he starts school, it is time to visit him.

If it is September and you want to go to an RV rally, it is time to travel on.

If it is October and you want to see the fall leaves in all their glory, it is time to go to Vermont and New Hamshire.

If it is November and soon will be December and you want to be with family for the Thanksgiving and Christmas holidays, you move to their hometown. But where do you move when your children are in North Carolina, Iowa, Texas and Alaska?

Chapter Three

RV Lifestyle Challenges
- Hairdresser

My favorite hairdresser, Sandy, was far away in North Carolina when I needed a haircut. I did not know where to go in the small town where we were in Arizona. So I drove up and down the streets looking for a beauty shop when I saw a small building that had "Wendy's Cuts" and a phone number written on the sign in front. I drove around the block before I decided to stop and see if I could make an appointment. There was only one word was on the door- "OPEN." Then I saw the letters that read "K-9."

The first thought I had was, "Kindergarten through 9th grade." "That's weird," I thought. This must be a children's hairdresser." I went to an inner door before I saw the picture of a dog. Duh, K-9 meant canine.

Pharmacy

Rod was sitting around the campfire when he told us about his experiences visiting a pharmacy in a little town in Arizona. Since his wife, Linda, has a chronic health problem, he often has to get prescription medicines while traveling. Sometimes the pharmacy doesn't have the medicines on hand or only a fraction of what is needed. They fill the amount of pills or liquids they can and charge him for all of them as they explain that he can pick up the rest in a week. That is not a good solution if you plan to move your RV to another site.

Rod once gave the well-dressed woman in the pharmacy a list of the medicines he wanted along with the quantity.

"Do you have these medicines here at the pharmacy?" Rod inquired.

"You need a prescription for them," she answered.

Again Rod asked "Do you have enough of these medicines in this pharmacy?"

Her voice was louder. "You need a prescription."

A third time Rod asked, "I know that but I need to know if you have the correct quantities on hand."

She was getting angry now. She yelled, "I told you. We

need a prescription!"

The owner of the pharmacy, with TOM written on his lab coat, came to help. "We have six gallons of that liquid stuff if you want it. We also have the other medicines."

The woman told her boss "I keep telling him that he needs a prescription."

Tom ignored her. "May I help you?" he said to Rod.

Rod gave him the phone number of the doctor that had prescribed the meds so Tom could get a fax of the prescription. Rod got the medicine for his wife.

Later Rod saw Tom in town. "You are married to the woman pharmacist, aren't you?" Rod asked.

Tom answered by nodding his head affirmatively.

Rod smiled. "I knew that. If she were just an employee, you would have fired her by now."

-Your Space

We are not used to sharing a bathroom with anyone else.

We were traveling with my parents to see Uncle Don in Arizona when my husband got up at 1am to go the bathroom. As he put his hand on the bathroom doorknob to open it, he saw a figure with white hair dressed in a white gown exiting the bathroom. He screamed. She screamed. Terry laughed when he discovered that the "ghost" was my mother dressed in her white nightgown. Lights went on and mumbled voices were heard in the area around us. I expected someone to call 911 for a law officer to check to see if everyone was all right.

———

My friend, Lois, was complaining that her husband, Mac, always put things in different places in the RV and she couldn't find them.

"We've solved that problem," I explained. "Terry is in charge of everything that goes into the belly of the whale" (our basement RV storage). When I want something, I say "Honey, find it for me."

Terry walked by and remarked "She really says- go fetch."

Lois quickly responded, "Does she give you a treat too?"

Terry blushed and said "Yes."

- Churches

Our grandson, Joshua, was about five years old when I heard his bedtime prayer. He concluded with "and may all the people in the world come to Pleasantville Baptist Church." I couldn't help laughing. So he wouldn't think that he had done sometime wrong, I told him that he had a good idea but there are too many people in the world to line up to go to his church. I added that God is in many different churches.

We can no longer go to our familiar church in our hometown so we visit places of worship on Sunday in whatever town or village where we happen to be visiting. Some buildings and furnishings are very different from what we are accustomed to. Some churches are picture book pretty with white clapboards and a bell in a white steeple overlooking a valley or river. Some have stained glass windows and tall spires. We saw "the little brown church in the dell." The Crystal Cathedral in California is shaped like an airplane made of glass windows with spires. We visited a church in Alaska where the warehouse exterior had not been renovated but the inside had beautiful scenic murals and plush carpeting. The log cabin in Nenana, Alaska had a beautiful altar cloth of beads woven on moose skin.

Sometimes we do not meet in a building. In Valdez, Alaska we were welcomed aboard a cruise ship called the "Lula Belle" and taken into the Prince William Sound where we sang familiar songs including one about us all being a part of the family of God.

We also met one Sunday in an outdoor service where we sat on a plank set on tree stumps. It was during a Rendezvous of the War of 1812. Most of the congregation were wearing clothing of the 1812 era. The minister read the 23rd Psalm and spoke of an unchanging God and that the Bible was "period correct" for today as well as centuries past.

The oldest churches that we have visited were the missions in California and the Russian Orthodox churches in Alaska. You will notice icons and candles used during their services. If you plan to attend a Russian Orthodox Church be prepared to stand for the entire hour and a half service.

We have heard beautiful organ music, acappella sing-ing, a full jazz band, a hillbilly guitar and banjo and a harpist. The music is as varied as a soft prayer to what can best be described as a joyful noise.

Sometimes we attend a campground church service and wear our usual slacks and T-shirts. Sometimes we attend church with other RV club members and ask what they wear. I have a favorite navy blue and white dress that I usually wear to a more formal church. No one knows or cares if I wear the same dress Sunday after Sunday. In a Western US church of about 150 people the minister wore blue jeans and a Western cowboy shirt. You might not want to wear a red dress to a Salvation Army Church. Most of the congregation wear navy blue or black uniforms.

We have gone to churches where the congregation num-bered in the thousands to one where it numbered six plus a barn swallow. (The bird flew erratically trying to get out of church but settled down when the service began.)

An advantage of a huge church is that you have so many talented people as resources for great music and drama. At the Crystal Cathedral, we attended the "Glory of Easter". The cast included hundreds of people and many live animals. The setting was Jerusalem. The time was the last week of Jesus life through the ascension. The costumes, choreography, and acting were so real that you felt that you were in a time warp. Using the same Hollywood technology that allowed Mary Martin to fly in "Peter Pan", angels were enabled to fly while the song "Alleluia" was heard. It was totally awesome.

I write about styles of church buildings, services, and what people wear. None of that really matters.

Worship is not about exterior things. It is about our attitudes and feelings as we reach toward God as He touches us.

———

The congregation of the Church of the Cove was sitting and chatting quietly in the campground clubhouse before the 9A.M. worship service. A gray-haired woman was reading the church program to her elderly husband. Like many husbands, he apparently was only half listening but whenever she paused, he would answer, "Okay."

The woman read, "We gather together following our church service for Sunday Brunch. We meet between 10:30 and 10:45 at Paradise Café. All are welcome to join us in Paradise."

The husband said, "Okay."

The wife queried, "Is it Okay with you for us to meet them at Paradise."

Her husband answered, "Yes, but you would think that they would ask us to meet them at church next Sunday and not wait until we get to heaven."

-Laundromat

For 37 years, I did my laundry at home. My RV lifestyle meant that I had to go to a laundromat. Here are some of the things that I have seen or have happened to me.

You are in Texas and can't find the laundromat so you stop at a gas station to ask where it is.

"Y'all parked in front of it, Ma'am." The gas station attendant looks at you like you have lost your marbles. Then you see a small sign to the right of the building that reads "WASHATERIA."

You put the detergent, bleach and clothes in the machine and deposit the money in the left-hand side of the machine. The machine to your right, where there are no clothes, turns on.

You set your liquid detergent on the top of the washer to remind you which machine you are using. After the clothes are laundered, you remove the detergent bottle. **It spills.**

You put your clothes in the dryer being careful to put the money in the top dryer slot. After they dry, you find an extra sock and t-shirt that doesn't belong to your family.

You fold the clothes and find out that the sock is yours. It is a different color because it got in the machine with the bleach.

Liquid soap flows all over the top and seeps into the machine onto your freshly washed laundry. The attendant appears. He says that the only thing you can do is wash your clothes all over again.

The attendant catches you trying to crawl into the washing machine. He comes over and asks, "What are you doing?" You explain that you are trying to get your bra out of the machine but the hooks are caught in the little holes in the cylinder.

You leave the laundromat and travel 17 miles to your RV and then discover that you left your jacket at the laundromat.

You are so tired that you go to bed. The next morning you can't get your arm out of the sleeve of your pajamas. You tug on it and discover a wad of gum is the adhesive that is sticking your arm to your nightclothes. The gum must have been in the clothes dryer at the laundromat.

- Food

Most food can be prepared in an RV- if you want to. Some husbands now do more cooking. Grilling is done more often since you are spending more time outdoors and have more leisure time. Restaurant food is always an option. Some people find, if they eat in restaurants most of the time, they eat larger portions. To avoid getting so big that you won't fit into your chair, you either take home the leftovers or you cook at home.

If you are looking for a barbeque sandwich in North Carolina, you will find a pork sandwich with a vinegary sauce and they will ask you if you want cole slaw on your sandwich.

If you are looking for a barbeque sandwich in Texas,

you will find a beef sandwich with a sweet, tomato flavored sauce and they will ask you if you want jalapeno peppers on it.

If you ask for a barbeque sandwich in Iowa, they will give you a grilled sandwich and ask you if you want catsup on it.

––––––

One of the more popular potluck meals is an egg breakfast. Sometimes instead of pot luck, the hostess requests you to sign up to bring cheese, bacon pieces, peppers, onion, olives, sour cream, tomatoes or some kind of breakfast bread and your eggs in a plastic freezer bag. You add ingredients into the freezer bag, which gets dumped into a roaster pan filled with boiling water. Presto- you have an omelet.

Pat asked, "What kind of eggs?" Someone answered, "Any kind of eggs." Del asked Pat," What kind of eggs do you want?" Pat answered, "Turtle eggs."

Del bought some little round brown mushrooms and cut the stems off. Then he sautéed them in bacon grease. They rolled into a little ball. Del did not think that they were brown enough so he added a little Kitchen Bouquet spice. Now they looked brown and a little slimy. He wrapped them in plastic wrap, put them into a freezer bag and offered them to Pat. She didn't think they were edible. So he added them to his and his wife's bags of food. Pat thought they were crazy.

––––––

Frank used to get his morning coffee at work. His solution to the coffee problem in the RV was to use the coffee bags on a string that make one cup of coffee in the same way you can make one cup of tea from a tea bag. He went into the country store at the campground to buy more bags.

"We don't stock them because they are too expensive," the clerk said.

"My wife, Opal, doesn't like coffee and doesn't know how to make it," was Frank's answer. "It would be much more expensive to replace Opal. It is cheaper for me to go into a restaurant and order a cup of hot water and a small Styrofoam box with my meal."

The clerk looked at Frank and asked, "Why do you want the box?"

"To save the coffee bag in it so I can take it home to make another cup of coffee," Frank explained.

———

Now you may think that finding a bakery is an easy task but to my husband it's an important one. He likes donuts.

Don's Donuts and Susie's Sweets were two donut shops in a small town in Texas.

Don advertised in the newspaper that his donuts were lower in price and lower in calories than anyone in the county. Susie just had to get the recipe. She sent her friend, Judy to buy donuts and see what she could learn. Judy put her whole heart into the project and accepted several dates with Don before she learned Don's secret. It wasn't the recipe that made the difference. Don just made his donuts smaller.

Susie went crazy trying to figure out how to stay in competition so she made the holes bigger in the donuts. The problem was that the larger the holes, the more dough it took to go around them.

———

The first drive-in bakery was managed by a real dough nut!

———

Sign in Quartzsite Bakery:

GET YOUR BUNS IN HERE.

———

How old are your canned goods? If they have 50 or 60 thousand miles on them either throw them out or give them away.

Happy Hour

before Rving   after RVing

before RVing	after RVing
Flower arrangements from local florist	Plastic bunch of roses
Tablecloth linen - freshly pressed	Tablecloth - plastic with checks
Crystal goblets	Plastic glasses
Sterling silver flatwear	Stainless steel with plastic for extras
Candles	Candles
Atmosphere of elegance	Atmosphere of laughter
Conversation about work	Conversation about where you've been and where you are going

Chapter Four

Finding Your Way and Mechanical Challenges

I am mechanically challenged. I am mechanically inept. Part of my problem is that I don't know my right hand from my left. (I married my husband by putting the ring on the finger of his right hand.)

I have learned that I wear my wedding ring on my left hand, so I am sometimes right. I get confused when I face Terry because my right is my husband's left. He has given up understanding what I mean when I'm right, so we just use driver's side and passenger's side when explaining directions to him.

Have you ever been lost? I was driving my toad (towed) car to take the short cut to my parents' house from my brother's elk ranch. I knew that I needed to travel north and east on gravel roads. I lived about 35 miles northwest when I lived in Iowa 25 years ago. If I crossed the Des Moines River, I was too far east of my route. My goal was the paved road G71 that crossed the intersection where my parents live between the town of Bussey and the intersection of Highway 63. If I went to Osky (Oskaloosa), I was too far east and north.

You may think that Iowa is pretty flat but you are thinking of Iowa north of Interstate 80. There are pretty steep hills in southern Iowa so you can't see very far in the horizon.

I thought that the Iowa roads were laid out in a grid. My problem was I kept coming to T-intersections. Often there was a sign that read "Dead End." I had no choice but to go the other way.

I must have traveled 15 or 20 miles between cornfields and fence posts with only an occasional homestead. There wasn't a cloud in the sky. Cows were lying under oak and maple trees or wading in a pond. It was too hot for them to chew their cud. Sometimes I saw a dead deer lying at the edge of the dusty road.

I knew that **I was in trouble** when the first town that I came to was Avery. I have never been in Avery before! There wasn't a person outdoors for me to ask directions. It was too hot. I traveled on.

Letters and numbers name most rural roads. I was on H27. I did not find Hoot Owl Hollow but I knew that **I was really in trouble** when I reached Whiskey Ridge.

It was a relief to see a water tower in the distance. Maybe I could get help in this town. In a grassy fenced-in area, the water tower read Wapello County Rural Water. My brothers live in Monroe County. My parents live in Mahaska County. I was in the wrong county! It was time for me to knock on the door of the next farmhouse even if I woke them up from their Sunday nap.

I told the farmer that I was from Texas and admitted to being lost. I needed to find Bussey or Oskaloosa. The farmer scratched his head.

"You are closer to Ottumwa," he explained. "Go back to the water tower and turn right. When you come to a T-road, turn left. At the next 2 T-roads, turn right. You will be in Chillicothe. After you cross the river, you will be on Highway 63."

"The Des Moines River, right?" I asked. He nodded his head.

No, I did not tell him that I have a problem with right and left. His facial expression already told me that he thought that I was not too smart. I thanked him and proceeded on.

I found Chillicothe and Highway 63 and G71. Instead of 23 miles, I had traveled over 50 miles to my parent's house. I took the paved roads home to my RV and called my mother when I got back to the camper, so she wouldn't worry.

———

It didn't use to bother me that I had a problem with mechanical things. I had a husband and sons to do the dirty work. Terry was trained as an engineer and is very good at fixing things but now I sometimes want to do somethings for myself.

Sometimes you just need to be taught how to do things.

Robbie said that she met some young campers who earned a trip by exchanging some labor for the use of an old RV. When Robbie asked how they liked RVing, they answered that the only problem was trying to line up the sewer hole to the dump's hole. It left such a mess!

Robbie's husband showed them the hose that was used for the job. They thought that using the hose was a wonderful improvement.

Jim told us about towing his car when he saw a car "just like theirs" passing them on the left. The car stopped but there was no one in it. It was their car that had come unconnected.

Sue responded, "We were traveling in our RV and towing our purple Cherokee with a yellow stripe. The Cherokee passed us. How many purple Cherokees do you see with a yellow stripe? We got so upset that we had to change our underwear. We pulled to a stop and guess what? Our toad (towed) was fine. We had seen another car just like ours."

Diane said that they unhooked their toad while it was in neutral. They did not have a problem until they unhooked it while on a slant. It rolled across the road up the incline to the freeway and then rolled back toward the road again and stopped in the ditch by the road. The funny part was both of them chasing the car as they tried to catch it.

———

Phyllis yelled for help to tie down her awning when the wind was bouncing it up and down. She told Bob to tie it to her car. He tied it to the wheel. Bob also told her not to drive away in the morning with the awning attached. Phyllis didn't drive away but the next morning her hubcap was up a tree.

———

Since you are not allowed to put your own fuel in your fuel tank in Oregon, a woman drove her tow truck to a service station and told the attendant that she wanted a dollar's worth of fuel.

"What do you want to do with it, lady?" the attendant said, "Do you want to smell it or put it behind your ear?"

———

A recent widow decided that she was going to solo RV. She did quite well when she drove the motorhome down the road. Then she proceeded to try to park in a crowded campground. She couldn't make it, so she tried again. She couldn't make it, so she drove around the campground and tried again a third time. After a third failed attempt, she put her head down on the steering wheel and cried. Charlie came up and said that he used to drive semis. Could he help? She nodded "Yes." He got behind the steering wheel and asked her to sit in the passenger's seat. Charlie scratched his head and grinned. How could he make her feel better? "Lady," he announced. "That was the best job of paralyzed parking that I ever seen."

Betsy says that watching other people park is often the best recreation in a campground.

———

Gene and Martha left Red Bay, Labrador just in time to get in line to catch the ferry to Newfoundland. A tour bus was in front of them. A man walked over and said, "Your rear tire is almost flat."

Sure enough, it was almost flat. Gene got out the jack, loosened the lug nuts, jacked the truck up, cranked the spare tire down and got it ready to put on. He took off the lug nuts and the flat tire, jacked the truck higher, and put the spare tire on. Then he lowered the truck, put the spare tire and jack in the back and proceeded to hurry on the ferry just before the ferry raised the back up and left port.

He was in agony because the disk in his back was pinching nerves going down his left leg and causing his muscles to spasm into knots. Carefully, he walked up the three flights of stairs to the lounge in front of the ferry and fell into a chair.

The comments from the bus tour were varied.

Gene had provided the entertainment for the day. Even his wife, Martha, had taken pictures.

"We are glad you made it."

"We took pictures of you changing the tire."

"We were cheering for you."

Gene had provided the entertainment for the day. Even his wife, Martha, had taken pictures.

When he told us the story, he ended with, "Why wasn't she selling tickets?"

―――――

You know that you are a happy camper when your RV is parked safely. Usually, it takes two people to line the RV up and park it correctly. One couple was late to get to the campground so they picked a vacant spot and attempted to park it in the dark. After much backing up and going forward, the woman yelled, "Stop! You are going to park it in the bushes."

The next morning, as they looked into the deep ravine, they realized that the bushes were not really bushes but treetops.

―――――

Kitty and her husband were traveling in the mountains in their medium-sized Class C motor home. In the valley, they passed a teeny tiny RV. Kitty's RV climbed the next mountain but vapor locked just before they reached the summit. As they waited for their RV to become unvapor locked, the teeny tiny RV passed them. This happened again and again as they played a game called the Tortoise and the Hare.

Chapter Five

Kids, Grandkids, and Other Relatives

Have you ever wanted to treat your kids as they have treated you?

Go to their refrigerator and open the door and just stare at what is inside. When they ask you what you are looking for, just answer, "I'm just looking."

When you are parked in their driveway, wait until they leave and throw a party in their house.

Don't worry about it when they say, "But we can never find you".

Answer "nowhere" when they ask, "Where are you now?"

One thing that is nice to do at your kid's house is to take them all your dirty laundry.

Do you ask them, "What's for dinner?"

Have your kids asked you lately when you are ready to settle down?

Do they say that they are glad to see you but do not have time to spend with you when you arrive?

Our friends, Wanda and Dexter, have told us that the best sight in the world is to see the headlights when their children and grandchildren arrive to visit. After a few days, the best thing is to see the taillights as they leave.

A good way to get revenge on your kids is to give the grandkids all kinds of noisy gifts like whistles and drums. You might want to wait until you are ready to leave the grandkids and travel on.

————

The best thing that our children have done is give us grandchildren! Aren't they wonderful? You can claim them as your family but are not responsible for them. My grandchildren are so smart!

They seem to size us up quickly. I spent the day with my granddaughter, Victoria, when she was five-and-a-half years old. She had not seen me since she was four-and-a-half. That night, she looked at me and said, "You like everything, laugh a lot and think that everything is funny."

They soon learn that Grandma's rules are different than Mom's rules. Grandma's rule is "You do what I want you to do and then we will do what you want to do. Many things we do together."

Victoria helped me make the "best waffles she had ever made." We watched cartoons together. We went to the Dollar store and the supermarket. She wanted to put the Barbie and Ken dolls to bed so I sewed them sleeping bags.

Their world is different than our world was at their age. They have never seen anyone hang clothes on a clothesline, listen to a record, or use a handkerchief.

———

One day, I saw a horrible expression on Victoria's face.

"What is the matter?" I solicitously inquired.

"Grandpa is utterly disgusting," she declared.

"What did he do?" I was curious now.

"He blew his nose in a piece of cloth and put it in his pocket." Victoria explained.

"He saves it," I remarked.

———

A grandson was asked, "If you stand with your back to the north and your face to the south, what would be on your left hand?"

He wasn't sure which was east or west so he looked up to his grandfather, grinned and answered "Your fingers." He was directionally challenged. Isn't it surprising that they are like us?

———

The six-year-old granddaughter jumped up the steps into the RV. As she wandered around, her eyes searched the interior.

"Itsy bitsy living room, itsy bitsy dining room, itsy bitsy kitchen, itsy bitsy bathroom, itsy bitsy bedroom." She whispered, "Grandma, you're not itsy bitsy". More diplomatically she added, "Don't you need a bigger house?"

Grandma smiled. "I have itsy bitsy dusting, vacuuming, and mopping to do. I can also park my house near the mall, the zoo, in the mountains and near the ocean and I can bring my house in your yard to see you. Do you want to help me make lunch?"

———

Helen just had to have a Christmas tree even though there wasn't much room in the RV. Finally she moved the table sideways and desperately tried to push the tree in the space.

"I just can't get this sucker in here," she remarked.

Later she found her grandson, Brian, crawling around under the tree.

"What are you doing there?" she inquired.

Brian answered, "Trying to find the sucker."

My ten-year-old granddaughter, Kari, learned in school that the plural of wife is wives and the plural of knife is knives so she decided that the plural of gift must be gives. She wrote me that grandma has "no gives under the Christmas tree but if grandma will send gives then I (Kari) will send grandma some gives."

Back in the sixties, we thought that it was neat to be "COOL". Kari says that to be cool is to be "constipated, overweighted, out of style, and a loser." She said that she is "NOT COOL". She would not say if I am cool or not. My only comment is that I am not a loser! I won $3.75 playing pokeno.

My octogenarian mother decided to buy some new clothes.

"I couldn't find anything decent," She complained. " All the clothes had low necklines and waists on your hips. The signs said they were 'HOT'. If that's hot, I don't want to be hot!"

Six year old Emily came to visit us in our RV. She wanted to remember everything she did so she could tell her family. I suggested that we take pictures and that I would write down everything in a notebook. She dictated, "Grandma lives in a camper. I think a house is better than a camper. The RV got smaller and moved. We drive the RV so it can take a dump."

How can the same parents have a child as chatty as Emily and another child as quiet as Joshua?

Joshua is the middle of five children in his family. On Saturday, Joshua swam in the pool, played miniature golf, and used a paddle boat. Sunday morning, I asked him what he liked best about the campground. His answer was "talking to you." Was he giving me a snow job or did he like being the only child in grandpa and grandma's RV?

———

Nathan, age 3, wanted to play putt putt golf with his siblings and his grandmother. With the help of his 16-year-old sister, Amanda, he hit a hole in one on the first hole and a hole in two on the second hole. What he couldn't figure out was that grandma got a lot more turns to play than he did.

———

Doris' grandson, Denim, loves his big white dog. Doris and Clark had dog-sat with her on occasions. Last week the grandson called Doris on the phone and told her about 6 new puppies that arrived at their house. "So, grandma," Denim explained, "You are a great grandmother. Can you come to our house and take care of the puppies? My dog thinks that you did such a good job of taking care of her that she wants you to take care of her babies."

———

Doris took her grandchild to the bathroom. Neither of them could find the button to turn the water on to wash their hands. A little 4-or 5-year-old girl showed them how to do it. Doris said, "Thank you."

The petite little girl spoke in a gentle voice, "That's okay. When you get old, you do not know how to do some things!"

———

My mother and father stopped to eat at a restaurant during one of their trips to Michigan. Some small children distracted mother as they were leaving the restaurant. Fifty miles down the road; mother discovered that her purse was missing. She insisted that they return to the restaurant so dad reluctantly turned back. As they drove up to the restaurant, dad remarked, "While you are checking on your purse, see if my hat is there."

Both the hat and the purse were recovered.

———

Some states have slogans on their license plates. Iowa has the name of the county where the vehicle was licensed. Winnebago Industries is in Winnebago County. When we were in Forest City, Iowa Raymond made the remark, "The people here are very proud of Winnebago. They all have it on their license plates."

———

My granddaughter, Emily, was visiting our RV at my brother's elk ranch when my brother gave her our mail from his mailbox. "Where is your mailbox?" she asked us.

"We don't have one," I answered.

"How do you get your mail?" she inquired.

"Our mail is sent to Texas. When we want it, we email or telephone them to put it in an envelope and send it to wherever we are. Sometimes they mail it to a post office. It is called general delivery. Sometimes they mail it to someone's house."

By now, Emily was bored but she wanted the last word. "You just need lots and lots of mailboxes," she concluded.

———

Hoping that my mother would be proud of me, I told her about the volunteer work that I had done at the senior center in Gila Bend, Arizona.

"I was even put into the local newspaper," I bragged.

Mother quickly responded, "I hope that you had no trouble getting out of it."

Chapter Six

Husbands

A friend of mine from Raleigh, North Carolina thinks that it is all right to crititize as long as you say, "Bless his heart" afterward. Apparently it is a Southern thing since I have heard it in Texas too.

I have a husband. "Bless his heart."

My husband has many admirable qualities but some little things aggravate me no end. He wipes up his spills or a speck of dirt or a dead fly with whatever is handy which is usually a washcloth or dishcloth. I tried to teach him that there are many materials on hand such as napkins, paper towels, or rags in addition to washcloths and dishcloths. Then I proceeded to define the proper use for each item.

A dishcloth is a cloth for washing dishes. A paper towel is for wiping spills or cleaning a greasy dish. A paper napkin is used for wiping your face at a meal or for wiping your plate if you are low on water and the nearest water supply is miles away. But you do not use your napkin to wipe the dish if you are at a restaurant. A rag is for washing the RV or can be used to wipe up vinyl floors. A washcloth is to be used to wash your body. Baby wipes can also be used as washcloths if your water supply is very low.

Did I succeed in teaching him anything? You have to be kidding. It was like teaching an old dog new tricks. I somewhat solved the problem by buying lots of wash cloths and dish cloths. If I do not know when he has last used the cloth, I get a new one. "Bless his heart!"

———

My husband takes pictures of everything. When we went to the Mississinewa re-enactment, he took 359 pictures in three days. Now he has taken some very fine pictures. Some of his pictures have even been published. But when he takes pictures of me, he likes to focus on my hips or has the light focus on my glasses so that it appears that I have glaucoma. He loves to take pictures of me when my mouth is open and I'm putting food into it.

After I choked on my food in an effort to protest, he said "Don't worry, I can always delete it. When have I ever kept a picture of you that you didn't like?"

"When you showed Aunt Jean and Uncle Bern the pictures of our trip to Alaska," I responded. "That was an accident," he answered.

———

My husband likes everything neat and tidy. So, he

picks up after me and stores any books, magazines, and sewing, in the storage place that is called the black hole, the black pit or the belly of the whale. The salesmen who sell RVs call it the basement storage.

Whenever you can't find anything it is usually stored somewhere but of course it has shifted. Terry says that I am hopeless so I let him be in charge of that little detail of living.

My husband was trained as an engineer and worked on computers all of his working years. He needed to be methodical, orderly, and exacting.

———

When he drives our RV, he wants to know what the elevation is, the temperature indoors and outdoors, the temperature in the radiator and the engine, the amount of fuel in the spare tank, and how many degrees we are north, south, east and west.

Once, when I was driving a car behind him, I told him on the CB that I needed to stop for gas. He told me to go ahead and gas up and keep the receipt. (Don't I always?) He would drive slowly so I could catch up.

I gassed up. I drove a couple of miles. Terry was nowhere to be seen. I came to a construction area where the flagger had stopped all traffic. Terry was still nowhere to be seen. He didn't answer the CB.

I approached the flagger and asked if he saw a large white 5th wheel pulled by a green truck. He shrugged his shoulders and scratched his head. "Did it have a lot of gadgets on the dash?"

"Yes, that is my husband. Thank you." I answered.

He gets a trip planner to tell him his destination point. It is accurate within a tenth of a mile. Terry is pleased when a plan comes together. He hates detours, toll stations, construction zones and peak traffic times.

I want to know if we are on the right road and are we there yet.

———

Carol forgot her glasses. So she borrowed my husband's glasses to see the computer.

As the evening wore on they played a game of pass the glasses and neither one was drinking.

———

A friend who was a hostess at an Escapade Rally was overwhelmed at the quantity of handouts and the size of the audience.

"I was never so glad to see anyone when I saw Terry. I needed help!" she exclaimed.

"Oh, you used my husband," I teased.

She replied "Yes, but I did not use him up. He is yours now."

———

I really missed him when there was no one to turn on the water pump and I was standing in the shower and the water stopped. I missed him when I wanted to talk to him and there was no one there. When he was gone to help our son move to Alaska, I missed him. I didn't sit in his place at the table, sleep on the left side of our bed or go into the belly of the whale.

"Bless his heart!"

———

The Sunday school teacher asked "Does anyone know anyone who is perfect?"

Scott raised his hand.

The teacher was surprised. "Who do you know who is perfect?" she inquired.

Scott explained, "My wife's first husband."

———

Our kids didn't understand our lifestyle when we said that we stopped at a truck stop for our anniversary dinner.

How to Get Rid of Your Husband - For a Little While

One of the problems of RVing is that you have your partner with you 24 hours a day, seven days a week.

We have developed a pattern that allows us to work quite well together because we have been fulltiming since 1997. Each of us has jobs that we do best. I cook the meals and clean the inside of the RV and he fixes and repairs all mechanical and electronical stuff.

I stay out of the bathroom when he is in there. I don't go to the bedroom because he takes up all the space in the bathroom and the bedroom is on the other side.

He stays out of the kitchen when I am cooking because it is dangerous. If I am draining hot water off potatoes or frying an egg or chopping vegetables, I can't have him close by. We have a one-butt kitchen and he does not look out for my body parts.

Sometimes you need to be alone but it is hard to be alone in the small oblong box we call home.

Several women RVers met at Quartzsite and discussed how we could get rid of our husbands - for a little while.

A woman suggested that if he is handy at fixing things, you might volunteer his services to a solo woman who needs help- for a little while.

Since men have more trouble meeting new friends than women do, help him out by opening the hood of the pickup. Soon there will be men gathered around. If you are lucky, they will decide to do something together.

You could get out his fishing stuff - to clean it. He might get the hint and decide to try the local fishing hole.

You can ask him to walk the dog.

A suggestion was made to make him a sack lunch and tell him that you hoped he would be home in time for dinner at 6p.m.

I usually just go do laundry. That gives me a couple of hours of time.

Chapter Seven

Pets and Other Animals

Our nine-year-old grandson, Jake, was watching the seniors at a campground when he asked, "Grandma, why do these people treat their dogs like kids?"

The only answer I could think of was, "they love them."

I asked Ellen what answer I should have given him.

"You did okay," she responded. "Also remember that pets do not ask to borrow money, come home drunk or tell you that it is your fault that they have problems. They give you unconditional love."

Some RVers call themselves, "Mom" and "Dad" to their their pets. That lifestyle is fine but animals, like children, need to be fed, toileted, and exercised. You need to clean them and clean up after them. Please don't disturb your neighbors or your pets by leaving them alone too long in your rig.

———

I met Cleone and Dillon walking around the boondock area of Quartzsite known as Boomerville. Cleone is an RVer and Dillon is her Yorkipoo dog. Dillon likes to jump and get into things that are edible and non-edible. One day while his Mom and Dad were out of the RV, he found boxes of chocolates that Cleone had bought for gifts. Dillon chewed the corner of each box and tasted each chocolate. He discarded the foil wrapped candies and ate all the caramel ones.

Another day, he crunched the tube of the cat's fur ball medicine until it was empty and ate the whole thing. Later, Cleone noticed that every time that the dog sat down, he left a grease spot. It was so bad that Cleone had to put diapers on him.

———

Emily was six-years-old when she found a sure way to get new pets. She prays for them. Of course, she makes sure that her parents hear her pray. She prayed for a cat and received one. After the cat was run over by a car, Emily prayed and received another cat.

She had a fish with brilliant colored fins that everyone assumed was a male. It died. Emily prayed. Her mother, Connie, told Emily that they were going RVing soon and did not want to take fish with them. They were not going to buy her new fish. When they cleaned out the bottom of the fish tank, they found four tiny baby fish. Emily got her wish for a fish.

We love animals and other critters outside our rig. The bugling of an elk or the gobbling of a turkey or the howling of a coyote is music to our ears. My husband loves to stop and photograph any wild animal that we happen to see.

Outside of Edmonton, Canada, we saw a coyote sunning himself in a meadow. We went to the next exit, disconnected the car and drove back to see if we could photograph the coyote. Yes, it was still there. It did not seem to mind the traffic going by but it ran off when we stopped on the shoulder of the highway. He paused and looked at us interspersed with running and stopping. We got some excellent photos.

On a trip to Alaska, Terry stopped the car suddenly and said, "There is a moose, in the bush, by your side of the car. You photograph him."

I took the picture and remarked, "It wasn't very big."

Terry insisted that it was a big moose so I showed him the picture on the digital camera.

"That's not the right moose," He proceeded to take a picture of the mother moose. I had taken a picture of her calf.

We were driving from Fairbanks to Denali National Park

when I saw what looked like a dirty white grocery bag in a ditch along the road. I made a remark about trash along the road when the "bag" up-ended and a swan appeared.

———

We were parked in a remote area of Alaska when we were awakened by a loud scratching that sounded like finger-nails on a chalk board. Could it be a bear? The sound was coming from under our rig. Why would a bear be under the rig? My husband decided to make some noise. So he turned on the generator. The animal ran off. The next day we learned that a porcupine lived in the neighborhood. A trailer near us had most of its insulation stripped by the critter.

———

We were in Fairbanks when we asked where we would be likely to see wild animals. The ranger showed us where they had been sighted.

"You know they might not be there," she explained. "Yesterday we had a woman complain that we let the wild animals out too soon and she did not see any. I guess she thought they were behind fences until a gate was opened."

———

It is elementary reasoning that to see wild animals, it is best to go where they live. Travel off the main roads. Slow down. Hopefully they will be at home when you arrive.

Chapter Eight

Snowbirds

This article is reprinted from the September/October 2003 issue of *Escapees Magazine* from an article called *A Discourse on the Habits of Migratory Snowbirds.*

Snowbirds are migratory Homo sapiens. Most of this species are 55 years old or older in human years. Their plumage is very colorful and can be any color. The crest on the male of the species is quite sparse and is usually white to silver gray. However, the female crest and crown may be any shade from white to black, silver to brown, or even yellow or red. They appear to be well fed to the point that many are plump.

The migratory snowbird differs from the normal Homo sapiens in that their nests are located in portable birdhouses. Other names for these birdhouses are vans, campers, rigs, 5th wheels, class C's and class A's. They seem to like expandable sides to their birdhouses. Some have as many as 4 "slide outs". They have aversions to cages, aviaries, fences, or coops. One group even calls themselves Escapees. One was heard to say that he had "flown the coop". Others assured me that they had escaped the work patterns and lifestyle of their former habitats.

Snowbirds follow the weather conditions and move south when frost first hits the Highway. Most of them can be found south of Interstate 10 in the U. S. They have migrated from as far North as Alaska and the Provinces of Canada.

If irritated, or for no discernable reason, they move to another location. Sometimes the time span is only a week, but it can be as long as 6 months. In the summer, these birds return to their prior habitats to see how their chicks are doing or travel north to explore new territories.

Most snowbirds can be found in little rectangular spaces in a "park" or "resort". In good weather, they expand their habitat beneath awnings as they move tables, chairs, rugs, food and barbeque grills, to outdoor areas. They call their birdbaths "hot tubs", "Jacuzzis" or "pools."

Other snowbirds boondock on BLM (Bureau of Land Management), which are desert lands. You can tell them from the sound of their generators. However, there is a silent boondocker, which catches sunlight in units called solar panels.

Snowbirds have a propensity for fire. They gather round a fire for warmth, conversation, and to watch the incredible sunsets over the desert. I was invited to join them, after having donned their uniform of T-shirt, pants, and sweat shirt.

They have their own speech patterns. What I could translate of their chirping, was that they conversed about places to roost and sources of food. They are also concerned about the size and weight of objects that they bring to their nest.

Some snowbirds are very concerned with their pets. I saw a contraption made of a luggage carrier bottom with a plastic bag attached to carry the products they had scavenged. The top portion was made of a baby stroller complete with canopy. Inside this thing was a perky black dog wearing sunglasses.

If you find a group of snowbirds, visit them. They are a congenial and entertaining flock of birds.

Chapter Nine

Things to Beware of

- Memory Lapses

Your problems are somewhat different when you RV.
Remember when you parked your car at a mall and had problems finding it? Now you have problems finding your home when parked in a large grid type RV resort.

We wear a nametag at most RV club social functions. It helps us to remember who we are.

Do you keep tabs on your grocery-shopping cart by remembering what you put in it or do you take the nearest cart and claim your husband must have added things to it?

Does your husband ask why you bought beans again and you claim that he put them in the cart?

Do you remember the names and ages of your children or do you have to ask your grandchildren?

Do you have a place for your credit card charge slips or do you have to search all your pockets and purses to check if you bought that_____ when the bill comes in?

Do you have specific places in your RV for small items or do you just throw them in a drawer and claim it is messy because of the bumps and turns you made down the road?

- Campground Rules

Every campground has rules. Here is a composite of what I have learned.

Don't put mats or rugs on the grass. It gives the lawnmower a tummy ache.

All kids under 14 must take an adult to the pool with them. Your parents like to feel needed and it gives them another chance to yell at you!

It's okay to whistle at the girls at the pool. They may whistle back!

Quiet hours are 10pm till 9am. It is okay to sleep in. You are on vacation or retired!

Please do not leave your trash out overnight. The wild critters are on a diet!

TO PREVENT STINKING

Please pick up your doggie doo. Violators are required to clean up the dump station.

Please do not leave your baby's diapers in the bathroom. Take them to the dumpster.

Please do not leave your Depends in the bathroom. Take them to the dumpster.

Please flush the **"toylet!"**

Game time in the clubhouse is at 7pm. We have card games that any moron can play. Please join us!

For Men Only

Do you know why it takes so much time for women to get ready in the morning?

They brush their teeth, shave their legs and arm pits, shampoo their hair, apply cream rinse, apply shower gel, rinse, dry, and apply cream to skin, apply deodorant, comb and curl their hair, and pluck a stray eyelash from their chin. After all this brushing, shaving, shampooing, creaming, gelling, rinsing, deodorizing, drying, combing, curling and plucking; it is time to start putting on their makeup.

We Are Being Followed

I find that 99% of the RVers are caring and sharing people but sometimes we are being followed by someone who disappears before we can meet them. Sometimes it is months before we notice they are following us again but I have been accumulating information on them. I know their habits. Eventually, I may know their identity. Now I call them the "ugly RVers".

They drive different models of RVs so maybe they are transporting them for a company that repossesses RVs. I don't know if it is an accident or do they look for our RV to park far enough away so we won't know that we are followed?

Usually they operate in the dark. They speed through the campground at 40 MPH and even blow their horn. They leave at 5:30 am after revving their gas engine or leaving their diesel engine running for 15 minutes. By the time I get my pajamas changed, they are gone.

But I can see where they have been. They use the campground's shower and don't close the door or curtain so there is a wet or muddy area in the shower. They let their dog out before they leave the campground. He does his business beside my picnic table. You know that they plan to return if they leave their clothes in the laundry room washer or if their dog is shut up in their RV, barking all day. I went to use the hot tub and found something brown and frothy floating on it. I was told that it was chocolate ice cream but since I wasn't sure, I did not use the hot tub that day.

I have seen them when we went to Wal-mart, too. They park their rig close to the store and put out their slide and steps. I have even seen a grill set up beside their rig. I stopped to confront them once but no one was in the rig.

We were boondocking in the desert when I heard them at midnight with their generator booming.

I caught a glimpse of them once when they arrived at a site close to mine. The wife was screaming at the husband to stop but he kept on going. Then I saw their back as they were gazing up into a tree. The language they were using was frightening to hear. I decided this was not a good time to meet them. I did not want to get caught in any violence.

I really don't know what I would do if I met them except to tell them that I do not want them to follow me.

Chapter Ten

Time to Buy a New RV

We had seven good years in our 32-foot fifth wheel when it happened. Our RV shrunk. The cupboards were so full that every time we stopped the RV and opened the cupboard doors, we were greeted with an avalanche.

"Don't you think that we need a new RV?" I asked.

"Our RV is fine. You need to get rid of stuff," Terry emphatically stated.

I got rid of some stuff and brought up the subject another way. "Do you know that there are RVs with five slideouts?" I asked.

"Our RV doesn't have much power in the mountains but we will get along OK."

He would need a little convincing.

"Why are the plastic boxes of clothes on my side of the bed?" he asked one morning.

"You noticed." I replied.

"I noticed. Why are the plastic boxes on my side of the bed?"

"Because my shoes and books are on my side of the bed." I answered.

"I told you to get rid of the books," he replied.

I had to try another approach. "I read in an RV magazine that there are three reasons why people buy an RV," I explained.

"They think their RV is like an appliance under warranty. When it starts to cost money, it is time to get rid of it.

"Or they think it is like a mirror that reflects the owner in every way and now that it has flaws, it is time to dispose of it.

"The third reason is that their RV is like an endowment policy that you have invested in but now it isn't adequate for your needs."

"Are you trying to tell me that you want another RV?" he asked.

Bingo. I tried not to act too enthusiastic. "What do you think?" I inquired.

We went to the clubhouse for cinnamon rolls and coffee and met a newcomer who had a new RV. After I admitted that I admired their RV, they invited us to come look inside.

It was almost what I wanted our RV to look like.

Word got around the clubhouse that we were looking for a new or used RV. When I returned from the swimming pool, Terry was showing our RV to Jean.

When Jean left, I asked Terry what he was doing.

"I'm making a list of things to take off the RV before we sell it to Jean. Do you think that she wants the solar collectors or will she always be on full hook-ups?" he asked.

"We need to make a list of what we want in a RV," Terry added.

We wandered in and out and in and out of RV showrooms but nothing was really better organized than what we already had in our fifth wheel.

We saw a glamorous RV with thick carpet, ceramic kitchen floors, and sidewalls of a shiny hard surface. Mirrors were everywhere- on the ceiling, walls and even on the front of the refrigerator. Mood lights reflected the glitzy surfaces. I couldn't imagine living in it. I would be cleaning it all the time. But it would be good for a lot of laughs. Can you imagine stepping out of the shower and seeing your middle aged body in mirrors all around you ?

Terry went to the Internet. "I like the engine and transmission in this one. It is 36 feet long but it has a kitchen slide and you know that I'm afraid that the wear and tear of going in and out will rupture the gas line and the sink drain. The slide is only 19 inches wide. Another RV has a good floor plan but the ratings of safety and durability are only 60 to 70%. A third one has a big side-by-side refrigerator, an ice maker, and a washer/dryer but not much hanging space."

"Did you check the floor plan to see if the front door is lined up so you can see a person sitting on the commode from it?" I asked. That was one of the things that I did not like about our fifth wheel.

We found an RV with the engine and transmission that he wanted, plus a larger 33-inch slide for the dining-room table and sofa. It still had an 8-cubic-foot refrigerator but the icemaker took up half that space. There was no space for a computer.

The first problem was solved with a freezer/ refrigerator in the slide out space in the downstairs storage.

We solved the second problem by removing a J couch and inserting a computer table.

There is no perfect RV but with modifications, you can come close.

The experts tell you that when you have limited your choices to two or three RVs, you need to sit on the chairs and commode, stand in the shower, reach for the cupboards and lie on the bed to see which RV will be most comfortable for you.

Make sure that the bathroom is big enough. You don't want to start the morning like Kitty did. She sat on the commode to shave her legs. A few minutes later she backed into the commode to use it when she dicovered that the lid was still down. She jumped forward to put the lid up and hit her head on the door. She backed up again and sat on the cold porcelain. She had pulled up both lids

————

Sam walked into his friend's RV dealership in Arizona. His friend, Joe, and a customer were having a heated discussion over the value of an RV.

"I'm glad you came in, Sam. John, meet my friend Sam from Minnesota. Sam is also an RV dealer. I want his opinion on this RV. What is it worth? I'll leave it to him."

Sam didn't answer but turned on his heel and left the dealership. Two hours later Joe phoned him.

"Are you crazy or something? While I was there with a customer I asked for your opinion on the RV. Why did you run away without answering me?"

"Because," answered his friend, "I didn't know if you were talking about a sale or a trade-in."

Chapter Eleven

Moving into an RV

We had things to move. Boy, did we have stuff! We found stuff that we thought was in storage.

I thought that the easy way to move is to put both RVs together and carry things from one RV and place them in the proper places in the new RV. I took a drawer full of rolled-up socks and opened the drawer in the new RV and dumped them in and returned the drawer to the old RV.

Terry's idea of moving was to place everything in boxes. When the boxes were almost full, he put other things on top that would fit even if they belonged in another room in the RV.

I went to make a sandwich but I could not find the bread. It turned out that Terry had packed the salt and pepper too.

When we sold our house to our son, we put a storage building in the back yard to hold the things we could not part with. Some things we gave to our children. Some things we asked them to keep for us and to return some day if we ever got a larger residence. Pictures were kept at my daughter's home. Sometimes we go to our children's homes and visit our things.

An RV is only a traveling vehicle. To make it a home, you need to add color to the sterile, neutral colors that the decorator thinks that everyone wants. You need to add flowers, afghans, throw pillows, magazines, books, place mats, small rugs and a few pictures of your grandchildren.

Shopping for your RV is difficult because everything in the store that looks like it will fit in the RV is too big when you get it home. This is one thing my husband is right about-you need to measure everything.

Now my problem is to learn all the gismos and gee haws that make it work.

We had seen the RV with the slideout both in and out. We did not see it move. Since we had a fifth wheel with slideouts, we knew that all you needed to do was flip the switch. We flipped the switch. Suddenly a female voice came from somewhere. She says to be sure the lock arms are up and everything is out of the way.

Sometimes I think that it controls me like "*Smart House*" did in the movies.

I turn on the fan. It turns itself off. Okay, it was sprinkling rain outside.

The fan over the convection oven wouldn't turn off. I guess it was too hot.

The convection oven is programed for sensor reheat, sensor cook, compu boil, compu roast, compu bake and compu defrost.

We had friends that said that their RV was programmed to talk even more than ours. One night, when she got up out of bed and used the bathroom, a voice reminded her that the black tank was three fourths full. That was the last straw. They disconnected the voice.

Chapter Twelve

Ecology, Conservation and Recycling

Some boondockers have made energy efficiency into an art form. They know the wattage of every electrial appliance they own and how many gallons of water they use for each task. When they use their generators, propane gas, solar panels and solar cookers, they are very efficient. Some RVers are so efficient that they use the dishwater to mop the floor. The rinse water is used for bathing. All water used in the bathroom sink is caught in a bowl and used again to give the toilet a good flushing.

Of course, recycling is not new. Aunt Nellie used to get me clothes from Beverly which were again used by my sisters, Clara and Angie. Mom liked to buy some outfits which were identical except for the size. Poor Angie. First she would wear her dress. Then she would wear the identical dress from Clara. Finally she fit into the same style dress from me.

I recycled too. I bought every Buster Brown shirt that was made in the 70's and recycled them from Richard to Steven to Mark

Steven to Mark.

There are some differences in the way people recycle. Dennis and Dorothy get a large newspaper every day. They have a special recycling container for newspapers. When we stay by Jim and Lora's home, we recycle like they do. We take the labels off and wash out vegetable cans. Plastics are saved separately. Organic food waste is given to their animals to eat or used for making a compost pile.

My dad saves the seeds from especially hardy vegetables and uses it for seed for next year's garden. Mom checks her junk mail for blank areas, which she uses for scrap paper.

Iowans pay a deposit on their pop (soda) bottles and cans, which is refunded when they take them to the recycling center.

Do you know Rvers who recycle everything except their toilet paper? I know of several people who save the cardboard centers of the toilet tissue rolls. They use these centers as toys for their dog. When they become unraveled, they use this cardboard to start campfires.

I use plastic grocery bags to hold garbage. I have been informed that plastic grocery bags should not be burned in a campfire because the fumes may be carcinogenic. If all else fails, you can always take your garbage with you to visit family and add it to their garbage can.

Cathy told me that she recycles dust by driving her RV with the windows open. She claims that it is a good way to clean the RV.

Chapter Thirteen

Fun with RVing

It took longer to drive to the campground than we thought. The weather was rainy and windy. Stuck in peak traffic, we came to a construction zone. "Why did we ever want to RV?" we asked each other. Whenever we hit the chuckholes, it is easy to forget what we love about camping. No, we don't chuckle through the chuckholes. It is later, when we recall our mishaps, that we smile and even laugh out loud. Then we remember why we wanted to RV in the first place.

We can go where we want when we want and we always have a clean, comfortable bed, food in our pantry, clothes hanging in a closet, and our toys with us.

How else can you afford to visit a grandchild and travel to Disneyworld and see the sights that make you young?

We like to take our 4 wheel drive car up an old road and go to the end.

Other favorite RV pastimes are going to a potluck dinner or sitting round a campfire with friends old and new.

We love the breathtaking scenery in all parts of North America. We have seen the majestic scenery of Alaska. We have photographed panoramic views in a full circle but when we show them to others; they see with tunnel vision what we have seen in reality.

RVing allows us to visit a National Monument one day and go on a fishing trip the next day.

During a family health crisis, we were parked in my family's yard. Yet we had our privacy.

———

We meet many people at campgrounds that have become our friends and playmates. I'll never forget the fun I had dressing up as a clown at an RV Rally. Our skit was about setting a world record with the most balloons in the air at the same time. The balloons had a gizmo in the bottom that made them spin and twirl as they buzzed toward the ceiling. In the skit, the photographer goofed so there was no world record. We clowns handed out balloons and helped blow them up.

The expressions on the white haired and bald audience were funny. The boy's choir, who were waiting to entertain us, watched from the sidelines but were not given balloons. The expressions on their faces as they watched the seniors at play varied from yearning to be part of the festivities to incredibility that the seniors were acting like children.

Fun and adventure mean different things to different folks.

You can go	checking historical data
hiking and biking,	**and**
rafting and crafting,	**anything**
fishing and wishing,	**else**
beading and reading,	**that**
writing and animal sighting,	**matters**
4 wheeling and RV dealing,	**to**
shopping and restaurant hopping	**you!**

If you are a woman and want to laugh and have fun become a Red Hat Lady.

The only rules are that:

1.You wear a red hat and purple clothes if you are fifty or older and you wear lavender and pink if you are under fifty.

2. You must smile and have fun. You can't be blue when you are wearing purple and red.

Red hats, bonnets, caps, and visors decorated with red and purple feathers, veiling, flowers, ribbons and bows made vivid scenes at an RV rally on Red Hat Day. Red and purple t-shirts, blouses, shorts, pants, capris, skirts, and dresses made up the remainder of their outfits. Accessories included necklaces, earrings, pins, feather boas, scarves, belts, and even Mardi gras beads. Some outfits were elaborate handmade creations. Others were quickly assembled from purchases at Wal-Mart or thrift shops. I even heard one woman say that she had purchased her t-shirt from Super Valu Supermarket.

I asked the red hat ladies that I met after Red Hat Day at an RV rally how they felt when they were wearing red hats and purple outfits. The general reply was that you could "let it all hang out." One woman told me that she felt that she had to be the "perfect wife and mother," but that in her outfit she could "be herself again."

How do others feel about your red hats? A group of purple clad women wearing red hats really make an entrance into a room. People stop and look at you. They look away and then look again. Usually they smile. Men often have a twinkle in their eye and open doors for you.

I asked how does your family feel about you wearing a red hat and purple clothes?

One woman answered, "They don't know. You can only act like a kid, if your kids are not around."

One husband exclaimed, "ooh la la. How much do you

charge?" The answer was a "lifetime commitment."

Another red hatter said that she told her daughter about the red hats and now her daughter was wearing a pink hat and lavender outfit.

My daughter, Karol, telephoned me and asked me several questions. I talked with her for several minutes and then explained that she had five minutes more because I had to leave to lead a red hat parade. The phone was silent. A small voice whimpered, "And I asked you for advice?"

A woman reported that her red hat group charged each member five dollars a year. They used the money for a tea party at a nursing home. The residents smiled at their outfits and enjoyed their efforts to sing old songs.

On a trolley ride to the hospitality room, a woman smiled and said that she wanted to tell me a red hat story.

Her sister, Carol, wanted to join the red hat society. She bought a red hat but became very ill before she could join the red hatters. She saw a group in a restaurant and told them about Carol. They said that if she would give them an address, a few women would visit Carol. A few days later, seventeen red and purple clad women came to Carol's house.

They made her an honorary member of their group and presented her with a pair of red shoes. Carol's face was animated as she read the red hat poem. That was the last time that the sister saw animation on her sister's face. She died a few weeks later.

A Rver was trying on hats before "Red Hat Day" at an RV Rally.

"That hat looks great on you. It makes you look ten years younger," the sales woman commented.

The customer quickly took the hat off. "Then I don't want it!" She exclaimed.

"I can't afford to look ten years older every time I take my hat off."

———

Bingo is one of the favorite games for the seniors in our campground on Lake Conroe. Every Tuesday, they go to the senior center in Willis, Texas. Either a low cost meal is cooked by a local restaurant or they brown bag it.

I suppose bingo is a favorite because you will win something. Everyone wins. First you win a "nanner" or an apple or an orange. Then you progress to a can of vegetables or box of cereal. The third game has cakes and pies and bread. You play each game until most of the people have bingoed. If you are so unlucky that your numbers were not called, you can come up and pick from the few leftover goods.

The highlight of the year, for the Willis seniors, is the Montgomery County Fair Senior Citizen's Day in Texas. You get a goodie bag as you go in the door. A senior book with local services and phone numbers is included with such things as toothbrushes, microwaveable popcorn bags, those rubber things to help get jar lids off and candy. We made our way to the tables, which are decorated with candy.

You haven't heard anything until you hear seniors sound like children.

"I got a toothbrush."

" I didn't get one."

"This toothbrush is little and pink. Maybe I could give it to Jerry. I heard that he has only three teeth left."

"I did not want popcorn." "Want to trade?"

"The caramel is sticking to my dentures."

At one time the conversation got around to museums. "I don't like museums. I used to use some of the housekeeping things that you see there. What does that make me? A museum piece?"

"Remember when your car was a 2-door Chevy or Model A with 4 cylinders?" "We had a 1934 Chevy with a rumble seat with knee action".

"Do you remember Howdy Doody on TV?"

Over the loudspeaker came the announcement, "Will the lady who left her glasses in the bathroom, please come up and get them?"

The local high school band played old time songs from yellowed and crumpled sheet music. Charlie commented that the acoustics were terrible. He adjusted his hearing aid as he stood up and commented "You can hear better if you stand up."

Someone commented, "Do you hear from your belly button? It must be good for something."

The teenage Montgomery Fair Queen appeared wearing a red plaid shirt and tight jeans with an enormous belt buckle. Only in Texas have I seen a queen wearing a black cowboy hat with a tiara over the crown of the hat. She walked through the audience and was respectfully speaking to seniors and shaking their hands. A woman patted her husband on the knee. "Only in your dreams," she whispered.

The seniors had their own royalty. Each of the senior centers had their own king and queen. Now was the time for the choosing of the one king and one queen to rule over all the festivities. You voted by how much noise you made. You could use party noisemakers but horns from RVs were prohibited. We made a lot of noise but there was a tie.

Where was Charlie with his booming voice?

"I had to go potty. I couldn't wait to make noise."

The tie was broken and our campground candidates, Wayne and Kora were King and Queen of Montgomery County. Maybe it was because Charlie yelled the second time. Maybe it was because Irene hit a cooking pan with a wooden spoon so hard that the spoon broke.

———

The following article was first published in the *Escapees Magazine* in the March/April 2004 issue under the title *"V" is for Volunteering and "I" = Being Involved.*

A friend, who only travels on vacation, said to me that she could never travel all the time because she needed to feel "involved".

I pondered this for some time and even consulted a dictionary. To be involved means to enfold or envelop, to engage as a participant, to occupy absorbingly, to commit oneself emotionally, to connect, to have within or as a part of oneself, and to have an effect on.

While at Rainbow's End, (the Escapees RV Club headquarters) I inquired how other Escapees felt involved.

I met Bob while I was doing our laundry. He was sweeping the floor of the laundry. I told him that it looked good to see a man sweeping a floor. He told me that he is a Work Camper Program Trainee. His wife is a Host Program Trainee. They are working for 6 weeks at Escapees and are going to work at Rainbow Parks.

"Why?" I asked. He said that they had traveled for several years and now wanted to"participate."

I met Estelle as we rode to a Red Hat Society meeting with Luci. Estelle said that because she "talks all the time" she always feels connected.

She said that "mother never taught me not to talk to strangers. God sends the right people at the right time to encourage me especially when I am in a crisis. I also encourage others."

Estelle and her husband Doug also work at CARE as

volunteers. (CARE stands for Continuing Assistance for Retired Escapees.) The CARE facilities are located at Rainbow's End and "provide permanent or temporary help for members who are grounded due to illness, surgery, age or disabilities" according to a brochure about Rainbow's End. Participants live in their RV's while receiving personal and medical care.

Estelle and Doug each work 16 hours a week. Both of them cook or help in the kitchen. Doug also drives participants of CARE to appointments. Estelle said, "We are out in the world doing good things."

Gus seemed astonished at my question of how to feel involved. He answered "The answer is in one word that starts with a V-Volunteer."

After a support meeting, a 91-year-old man helped him put chairs away and asked him, "May I ask you a question? You do not have to answer but just think about it. Do you have a goal for your life after your wife dies?" Gus thought about it, went to an Escapees magazine and looked at the BOF (Birds of a Feather) groups. His hand went to Habitant for Humanity. He decided to build a two bedroom bungalow house in Livingston as a tribute/memorial to his wife, Happy, who had died on February 24, 2003. He also works for CARE.

Gus wrote me "Your question, in essence, was how being a volunteer enhances my life. The short answer is that volunteering keeps me busy with projects and people that I find fascinating and fun. Days fly by with no boredom and there is an abundance of appreciative people for whom I provide the volunteer services. The other volunteers in the HFH (Habitant for Humanity) building and I have bonded as it were. We are close friends doing the Lord's work for others."

I met Jim and Joyce at social hour at the activity center. They said they volunteered for SOWERS from Lindale, TX. They explained that SOWERS is an interdenominational group of Christians who work at churches, Christian schools, conference centers, and children's campgrounds for 24 hours a week. The work consists of building, remodeling, painting, cleaning, working in a gift shop, and decorating. They are furnished with full hookups for their RV.

When I asked how they felt involved, they answered using the words "fellowship," "camaraderie," "making life-time friends", "serving the Lord." Satisfaction is felt because some person or child is helped because of their work.

I met Loretta as we left happy hour at the Activity Center at Escapees. We discussed the jokes that Joe Peterson had read. "I needed the laughter," she said. She told me that she lives at CARE doing sewing. "I need to be needed."

I then told her about my quest for how to be involved. She responded that you also need to ask for help. Some people, like her husband, found it hard to ask for help. She repeated that to be connected you also have to ask for help.

Lawrence helped by driving us to Catfish Bill's on Dine Out Night at Escapees in Livingston.

John and Carol drove me to a concert in Livingston, featuring a blind country/gospel musician.

Dinah played a game of Scrabble with a CARE participant.

Tom and Kay gave a slide show over their trip to New Zeeland.

I attended a free basic skills computer class. My husband, Terry, shared information with several people at a more advanced computer meeting.

How can you become involved? You can become involved by playing games such as Mexican Train, hand and foot, or bingo. You can give someone a hug. You can volunteer. You can just talk with people. If you find it hard to talk, just go to your RV and lift the hood, or walk your dog or cat.

You will find people participating with you in no time.

———

Our RV friends are special friends. They understand us. They have been there and done that.

We see the same RVers again and again. We met Gene and Martha in Quartzsite, Arizona. When we said that we were going to Alaska in the summer, they told us that they also planned to go there. Six couples from the Boomer Club BOF of Escapees met in Fairbanks including Gene and Martha and Terry and me. Accidentally, we saw them again in Sidney, Nebraska at a sporting goods store. They spent some time with their family in 2004 in Greensboro, North Carolina. We stayed a couple of days at their son's house on our way to see our son in Raleigh. In 2005, we saw them again in Quartzsite.

Escapees have a tradition of hugging other Escapees when they meet along the way. Sometimes our RV friends have felt like extended family. For some RVers, other campers are the only family they have.

When we meet new RVers, we soon learn that we have been in the same places and know the same people. We were in California when I met a woman who said that she was going home to Kelowna, British Columbia for Easter. I told her that my first cousin lived there. She asked my cousin's name. I said Gladys Vis. What were the chances that she would know my cousin in a town as big as Kelowna? The woman told me that she would say "Hello" to Gladys on Easter since Gladys played the organ in their church.

You have to be careful what you say about people. Our RV friends might know them. You never know who they are talking about. It might even be you.

We were parked southeast of Quartzsite, Arizona with about 150 other Rvers when I met Johnny and Margaret Johnson. I decided to check the bulletin board, which listed all of our club activities of the week. Margaret and Johnny introduced themselves. Since I detected a southern accent, I asked where they were they were from.

"Swansboro, North Carolina." Margaret answered in a pleasant southern accent.

"We lived for ten years in Raleigh, North Carolina before we went fulltiming," I explained.

"There is another couple here from Raleigh. You should meet them, " Margaret said.

"I'd like that," I answered.

That night they were astonished to see my husband and myself sitting around the campfire.

"You are married to him?" Margaret asked.

"Yes," I acknowledged. They laughed.

Terry had helped them to purchase their solar components in town. The "other couple from Raleigh" was Terry and his wife. As Terry's wife, I was supposed to meet -me.

Chapter Fourteen

Special Tales From RVers
-Who are you?

We met Johnny and Margaret again and asked them to stay for dinner. During the conversation, they told us how they had met.

Johnny was in the Marine Corps stationed at Parris Island, South Carolina, in October 1966 when he decided to go on a double date to a dance. Margaret's girlfriend sat in the front seat with Johnny. Margaret was in the back seat with a guy with Russian hands and Roman fingers. She slapped her date so hard that Johnny heard it in the front seat.

Johnny thought that Margaret, the French girl with long naturally curly hair and blue eyes, was pretty cute. He asked her for a date. Margaret was shy and Johnny was cautious on their first date. He remembered the slap. Johnny hugged the driver's door and Margaret hugged the passenger's door in the car. They got to know each other a little better while they dated in November.

On December 4th, they had a date to celebrate Johnny's 21st birthday. Margaret was not feeling well but went anyway because she did not want to disappoint Johnny. Margaret got more and more ill until she could hardly stand. Johnny did not know what to do but suggested he take Margaret to Beaufort Memorial Hospital. Margaret agreed.

At the hospital, Margaret was diagnosed with kidney infection and appendicitis. She was placed in a ward with three other women. The nurse came into the room and announced that they had a problem. The hospital could not treat Margaret nor discharge her and they certainly could not operate on her since she was only 19 years old. The brother that Margaret was staying with could not be found. Her mother had died when she was fifteen. Her father, who spoke little English, was in Louisiana along with her sister. What should Margaret do?

"I know." The little lady who was a patient in the next bed interjected.

" Y'all are just going to have to get married. I know Judge Bushard. He was my boyfriend in second grade. You just go to his house and tell him that I said that you need to get married. Don't worry about the waiting period. He'll take care of that. Just tell him to be here at 9a.m. tomorrow morning."

Johnny was scared but he went to the address the little old lady gave him and explained the situation.

The next morning Johnny put on a suit and went to the hospital. He was so scared that he drove past the hospital but turned around and was there before 9a.m.

Judge Bushard arrived. Someone found a red negligee and red and gold slippers for the bride. Other patients brought their flowers into the ward.

Johnny said that "anyone who could walk, roll in a wheelchair or crawl came to the wedding. The room was full of people." Margaret and Johnny each filled out their paperwork. The judge was ready.

"Do you , Harold Wayne Johnson, take this woman. . .?" Margaret thought "**WHO?**" Was she getting married by proxy to someone else?

Johnny answered "I do."

Do you, Fedia Margaret Vallot, take this man . . ? Johnny thought "**WHO?**"

Margaret answered "I do."

Neither of them had thought to tell each other what their legal name was.

Later that day, December 6th, Margaret's brother came home and learned that Margaret was in the hospital. He arrived that night to check things out and ended the night sleeping at Johnny's apartment. Margaret spent her wedding night in the hospital.

Later that month, Johnny took his bride to meet his mother. She did not believe that her baby was married and insisted that they were not going to sleep together.

She even invited his old girlfriends over to visit before Johnny left to go overseas.

Johnny's family called him by his middle name- Wayne. Margaret talked to the family about Johnny and what they had been doing. His mother could not understand it.

"She sure has nerve talking about her boyfriend Johnny when she says that she is married to Wayne."

Johnny drove his wife from South Carolina to Louisiana to meet her father. Two months after the wedding, Johnny left Margaret in Louisiana for the 18 months he was stationed in Japan.

What chance did this marriage have? Two children and five grandchildren and 38 years later, Johnny and Margaret are happy campers.

———

Change of Heart

We met Dick and Sharon Bolle at an RV park in the desert of California and were surprised to see them a month later near San Bernardino at a steak dinner in the clubhouse.

Dick and Sharon were born and raised in Iowa. Since I have lived in Iowa longer than anywhere, we immediately found that we knew the same places and had common interests.

For the last thirty some years, they have lived in Texas.

They travel about half of the year in their RV and live on a lake the rest of the time. Their interests are canoeing, riding a tandem bike, exploring National Forests and RV manufacturers and eating in small restaurants where you don't recognize the name.

They mentioned that they were planning to visit an RV factory on Monday. Were we interested? We contacted the manufacturer and discovered that they had a 10 am Class A tour and a 3 pm Class C tour. We offered to drive and decided to eat lunch at a little restaurant without a national franchise.

We had a good time on Monday. We even did a little shopping after the tours. I was exhausted. Dick and Sharon never complained. They were unusually courteous. Dick chivalrously opened the car door for me.

Why is this couple so special? We meet RV people all the time who are like them. Maybe they don't ride tandem bikes or open car doors but most Rvers are pleasant people whom we have met again and again.

But Dick wasn't always like this. He has had a change of heart.

I don't mean that he was a bad guy who became a good guy. Dick was a very sick man who has had a heart transplant.

In 1980, Dr. Cooley gave him a new heart valve at St. Luke's Hospital in Houston, Texas. It improved his condition but gradually he became more and more ill until he was spending almost as much time in the hospital as out of it.

Dick and Sharon moved to Houston in 1987 to an apartment to await the news of an available heart. They were at the zoo when the pager went off. Sharon pushed Dick in the wheel chair to the phone to get the news. A heart was available. When the doctors and nurses heard where they were, Dick was called "the man from the zoo". While prepping Dick for surgery, the doctors learned that the heart was not suitable for Dick. Emotionally, he must have felt like a woman who is 9 months pregnant who goes to thehospital and is sent home again. You know that you will get this wonderful gift but not today.

He was called again on June 22, 1987 to receive the heart of a 19-year-old man. Emotionally, the time of surgery is more difficult for the close family members than for the patient. He is given pain meds and meds to make him unconscious while the family members can only wait and pray.

Sharon supported Dick all the way. She stayed with him and asked questions and checked everything done for him. Their marriage is like riding a tandem bike – supporting and balancing each other.

Dick worked as a person who developed and created prototypes for heating and air conditioning systems. His work was both mental and physical. He was able to return to work in January of 1988. He has now retired. Dick goes to St. Luke's Hospital for a yearly check-up.

Dick appreciates the gift of life. He especially appreciates that he is physically able to do as much as any 69-year-old man with a thirty-something heart.

Uncle Don

The first member of our family to fulltime - was Uncle Don. He was also the most romantic person in my young life. I don't mean the man/woman hearts and flowers meaning of the word but in the heroic, adventurous, remote, mysterious or idealized sense of the word.

Uncle Don left home while still a teenager and did not let his family know where he was living. As a young girl, I remember my father praying for him as he said grace before meals. Who was this famous or infamous man who seemed to live by no rules? Later we learned that he had gone to England during the time of WW II. So, of course, he had rules- military rules.

Ten years later when I answered the phone one day, a man's voice said he was Don. I immediately ran to get my father. He was in his room in the Quonset hut on our farm. We were told to never interrupt my father when he was writing a sermon but I just knew that dad needed to speak to Don-now. I heard him ask Don where he was. Father's face was pinched and white as he ran to the car and sped away breaking all speed limits.

We met Uncle Don then. He was a thin man as tall as my father and with my father's penetratingly blue eyes. He had no teeth but more hair than my father. He wore a black Stetson hat and smoked a pipe. He looked like a sinewy, slim cowboy I had seen on TV.

Don stayed in Michigan with his sister, Etta (Henrietta),

and her husband, John. He never talked much to me. He only spoke when just a few people were around. That was not at our house since I had five brothers and sisters at that time.

Later our family moved to Iowa and Don moved "out west".

Occasionally, he would phone my father or one of his other brothers' or sisters' homes. He said he was in Arizona, Wyoming, Oregon, or Montana. Sometimes he would drive his big truck and trailer to see his sister, Bernice, in Montana. He needed a medium duty truck because he was a rock hound. Besides prospecting for rocks and semi-precious stones, he sold rocks and jewelry.

In 1983, he told Bernice that he would be in Quartzsite, Arizona, in January at the Rock and Gem Festival. My father had not seen Don since 1956 when we moved to Iowa. That had been 27 years earlier.

Dad looked at the map. In 1983, Quartzsite, Arizona, was a small town of about 800 people. It shouldn't be hard to find Don's white truck.

"We are going to see Don," Dad announced to my mother. They left Iowa at the end of December and arrived in Quartzsite on New Year's Eve in 1983.

They drove in the desert and all around town for two hours bewildered by all the people.

Finally, they found an information building. The attendant explained that there were between 25,000 and 55,000 people in Quartzsite then. "Why do you want to find him?" the information attendant asked.

"He is my brother," Dad answered.

"I will help you look," he offered. "If you do not find him by 2 p.m. tomorrow, stop by to find out what I have learned.

Dad and Mom walked Main Street from the Main Event, past the Stagecoach restaurant toward McCloud's for two and a half hours.

Finally, they saw a thin man unloading a white truck. "That's him," Dad said.

"Hello Don."

Don continued to unload his truck. He did not know that anyone was looking for him.

"I don't know you," Don replied.

Dad stepped closer and gave him a big hug. Don looked into the blue eyes so like his own.

"Clarence?"

They had a happy reunion. Dad went to Quartzsite every two years after that to see Don.

After my husband and I retired, we met Don in Quartzsite with my parents. When my parents returned to their home, Don talked to me over the next few years about owning two airplanes, prospecting, his dogs, and about his military life.

Don was in the middle of the ocean when he was ordered to bake bread for the troops but the only flour on board was filled with bugs. There was no way to get more flour since they were in the middle of war and supplies were difficult to obtain. He thought about it. The troops needed to eat. Don figured that if the bugs were baked, they couldn't harm anyone. He added sugar to the mixture and told them that he was making sweet breads with ground up-raisins. Several men told him that they had never had better bread.

On August 6, 1945, Don was in the middle of the Pacific Ocean. He was bound for Japan to invade the coastline. The bomb fell on Hiroshima. The ship that Don was on turned back to the USA. "I would have died if we had not dropped that bomb," Don said in a subdued voice. "We never would have survived invading the Japanese coast."

Don almost got married but the woman to whom he proposed decided not to marry him. Why? She explained that Don might live with her in the winter but in the spring the gypsy in him would want to move. She did not want to RV but to stay in her little hometown.

Today, Don lives in an apartment in Oregon and does not go to Quartzsite. For me, Quartzsite is not the same without him.

———

It is sad when one partner wants to RV and the other one is not housebroken.

Chapter Fifteen

Lessons Learned From RVing

We carry too much stuff. The extra weight is hard on your RV. We carry too much stuff in our hearts too. The extra weight hurts us more than anything else.

Everyone needs a hug or pat on the back or compliment. Not everyone will give you one back but the more you give, the more you will receive.

Be proud of your country. There is so much to see and experience. It will take a lifetime. Even places you have seen are different in different seasons. The mountains look so different when you arrive from the other direction.

God does not live in one place of worship. If your heart has acceptance, faith, and love, blessings are all around you.

In everyone's life, some rain will fall. If the area is dry and dusty, rain is good. If it has rained for 40 days and 40 nights, you will probably get stuck.

RVing is more fun with a companion. It is especially fun when you both speak simultaneously, "Look at ____."

Heaven is where all the machines work. If you can't fix things, find someone who can. Better yet, marry that person.

Unless you know it is poison for you, try it. You might like it.

Slow down and linger awhile in one area. You can drive one mile across a state border and say you have been in that state but you will not have experienced it. You also save fuel by slowing down.

There are many kinds of RVs manufactured because people have many kinds of needs, wants and desires.

Most RVers are like you. They are doing their best to get from point A to point B. The sight of a mountainside covered by wild flowers in the spring or trees full of autumn leaves in the fall looks the same from a $300,000 RV as from a much used $10,000 RV.

Everytime that Uncle Don said "good-bye," he always added, "You kids have fun!"

What is your life worth? You have only a certain number of dollars and a certain number of days. How will you spend them?

RVing is about fulfilling dreams- in spite of the chuckholes.

See next page for ordering information.

RV Chuckles and Chuckholes - the Confessions of Happy Campers

Order information:

> **Mail: Roving Pen Publishing**
> Attention: Darlene Miller
> 230 Rainbow Drive
> # 13012
> Livingston, Texas 77399-2030

Phone: 503-440-4636
Email: rovingpen@Direcway.com

Multiply total number of copies:_____ by \$9.95 =
Total cost of books _____

Add \$2.50 for postage and handling for first book
and add 50-cents for each additional book.

> Shipping total _____
> Texas residents
> add 8.25 % sales tax_____

> Total order _____

number on check enclosed _____
Name_____
Address_____
City, State, Zip_____
Phone _____
Email _____